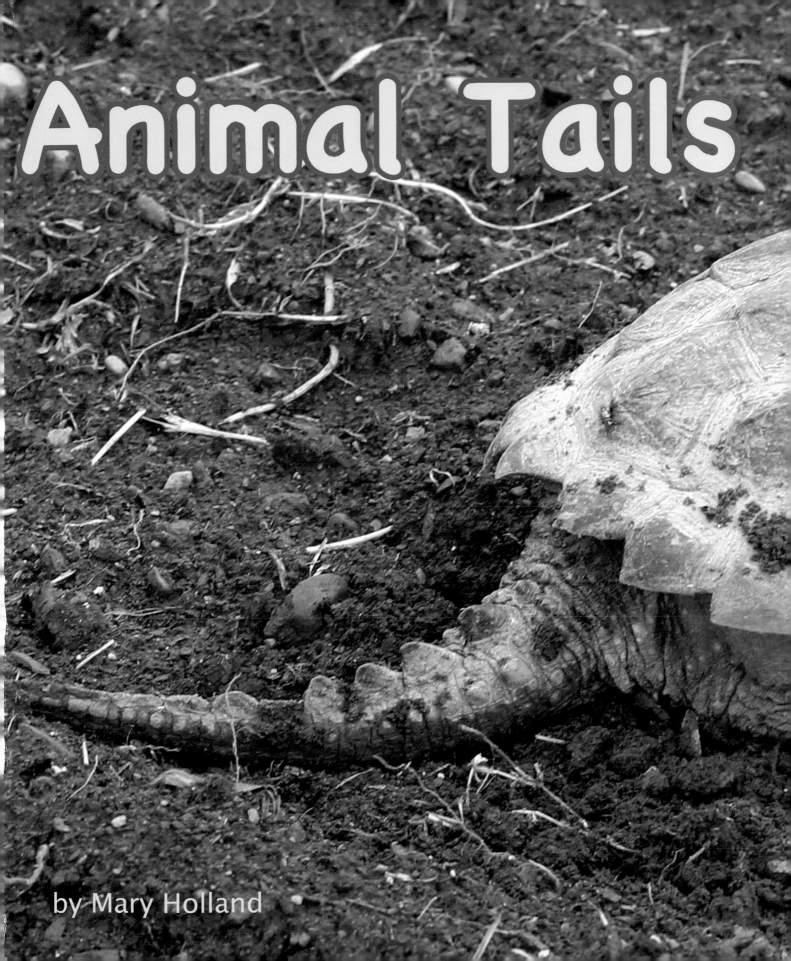

Animal Tails

by Mary Holland

Some animals have tails and some don't. Do you have one? Not anymore, but before you were born, you had one!

Tails come in all kinds of shapes, colors, and sizes. They help animals do many things: move on land, swim, warn others, steer, hold onto things, keep warm, balance, fly, attract a mate, and defend themselves.

There are animals that begin their life with a tail, but lose it by the time they grow up. This is true for most frogs and toads. They lay their eggs in the water. When the eggs hatch, the frog and toad tadpoles have tails.

What do you think their tails help them do?

Before a tadpole comes out of the water to live on land, it grows four legs. Its tail is absorbed by its body, and eventually disappears.

Some animals use their tails to signal other animals like themselves. Sometimes the signal means "*danger—run!*"

White-tailed deer have tails that are brown on top and white underneath. When a deer senses danger, it lifts its tail up so that the white hairs on the bottom of its tail show. The deer waves its tail like a flag as it runs away, warning other deer of the danger.

A beaver uses its tail to warn other beavers of danger. It slaps its tail on the water, which makes a loud sound that tells other beavers to swim to a safe place. A beaver uses its tail for other things as well: to store fat, to steer when it is swimming, and as a prop to rest against when it stands on its hind feet to cut down a tree.

Have you ever smelled a striped skunk's spray? It smells pretty bad. Spraying is a skunk's way of defending itself, but it doesn't spray unless it fears for its life. If an enemy (predator) is approaching, the first thing a striped skunk does is stamp its front feet on the ground. This tells the predator not to come any closer. If it keeps coming, the skunk lifts its tail, which is a signal that it is about to spray. If this doesn't stop the predator, the skunk turns around so that its rear end is pointing at the approaching predator. It then sprays an oily liquid that will not only make the predator smell bad for days and days, but will sting its eyes and give the skunk a chance to escape.

Some animals, like the Virginia opossum, have a tail that can hold onto things (prehensile). Opossums use their tail as a fifth leg. When an opossum climbs a tree, it grasps the tree trunk and branches with its tail as well as its feet. It also carries leaves and other nesting material in its tail.

If a tail is big and bushy enough, it can be used as a blanket to keep an animal warm when it is cold outside. In the winter, foxes and coyotes sleep out in the open, where it can be very windy and cold. When they go to sleep, they curl up and wrap their tails around them, tucking their noses down into their tails.

A bird's tail is like a boat's rudder. It helps the bird steer when it is flying. Without tails, many birds would find it hard to take off, turn, land, and perch. Tails help birds slow down as well as change direction when they are flying. They keep birds balanced when they are perched on a branch. Tails help catch the wind, which lifts birds high in the sky. Birds even spread out and display their tails to attract a mate.

This bald eagle is able to carry a big branch back to its nest because it can fly, and it can fly in the direction it wants to go because it has a tail.

Birds are not the only animals that use their tails to steer. Muskrats and beavers use their tails as rudders in the water.

A muskrat's tail is thin and covered with scales. The tail moves back and forth from side to side as a muskrat swims, both propelling and steering it.

Some birds, including woodpeckers, have very stiff tails. They use their tails to brace themselves against tree branches and trunks while perched. Because their tail supports them, woodpeckers don't become too wobbly when they are drilling for insects in a tree or making a nest hole (cavity).

Tails are used by many animals to protect themselves. A porcupine has sharp quills on its tail, as well as most of its body. These tail quills are shorter and thinner than most of a porcupine's quills, and will disappear quickly into another animal if the animal comes in contact with them.

Porcupines cannot shoot their quills. Often, when cornered, a porcupine will flick its tail at its enemy. If its tail touches the attacking animal, some of the quills will loosen and get stuck in the enemy's body—a very painful experience.

Some insects have tail-like structures at the tip of their abdomen. Female bees and wasps have stingers, earwigs have pincers, and female crickets have egg-laying tubes (ovipositors).

The sharp stinger of a female worker honey bee is covered with tiny, hooked barbs. If a honey bee stings someone, the honey bee will die. It does not use its stinger unless it is very scared. The queen bee also has a stinger, but hers is smooth, so she can sting more than once. She uses it mostly for laying eggs.

An insect called a tortoise beetle uses its tail-like appendage to protect itself from predators while it is growing up. The young tortoise beetle puts its old, shed skins, as well as its poop, onto tail-like spines (anal fork) at the end of its body. Then it holds the spines up over its back. This looks a bit like an umbrella and it protects the young beetle from predators that would like to eat it.

adult tortoise beetle

For Creative Minds

How Animals Use Their Tails

1 beaver

2 earwig

3 field cricket

4 coyote

5 red-tailed hawk

A   My tail helps me fly. My short, wide tail feathers catch the wind and let me steer as I soar through the sky.

B   My tail is for protecting myself. I have pincers on my tail to protect me from predators. Sometimes I use these pincers to attract a mate or fight over food with other animals like me.

C   I use my tail to keep warm at night. When the weather gets cold, I curl up and sleep with my nose tucked into my tail. The soft, fluffy fur helps me stay warm even in snowy weather.

D   I use my tail to lay eggs. I have a long, tube-like tail called an "ovipositor." This helps me lay my eggs inside plant stems or in the dirt.

E   *Smack.* My tail slaps against the water with a booming sound. Other animals like me hear the sound and know a threat is nearby. They dive for cover. When I swim, I use my tail to steer.

Answers: 1-E, 2-B, 3-D, 4-C, 5-A

Match the Tail

Match each animal with its tail. Answers are below.

mallard

painted turtle

flying squirrel

hairy-tailed mole

woodchuck

fisher

1

2

3

4

5

6

Answers: 1-woodchuck, 2-mallard, 3-fisher, 4-flying squirrel, 5-hairy-tailed mole, 6-painted turtle

Tail Adaptations

Adaptations help animals to live in their habitat. Adaptations help them to get food and water, to protect themselves from predators, to survive weather, and even to help them make their homes. Adaptations can be physical or behavioral.

Body parts, body coverings, and camouflage are all **physical adaptations**. A bat's ears are adapted so that it can listen for echoes to "see" its surroundings at night. A toad's brown, bumpy skin helps it blend in with soil and leaves.

Instincts and habits learned from other animals are **behavioral adaptations**. Some animals hibernate through the winter to conserve energy while other animals may migrate to warmer locations where they can find food. An opossum faints and looks like it is dead so predators won't eat it.

Are the animal tails in this section examples of physical or behavioral adaptations?

Even though they are called flying squirrels, these small rodents do not fly, or propel themselves through the air. Instead, they glide from a spot on one tree to a lower spot on another tree, or the ground. Flying squirrels run up a tree, jump into the air and stretch out their feet, using the flap of skin (patagium) that goes from their front feet to their hind feet as a parachute. While gliding downwards, they use their tail to keep from wobbling back and forth in the air and as a brake to slow down before they reach their landing spot. Flying squirrels can glide more than 150 feet in one glide.

Most salamanders have tails which they can shed when attacked by a predator. When the predator grabs a salamander by the tail, the tail separates from the salamander, allowing it to escape. The salamander's tail grows back in a few months. Sometimes a salamander's tail that has been shed will continue to wiggle, fooling the predator into watching it, rather than chasing after the salamander that shed it.

Salamanders that live in the water move their tails from side to side, propelling them through the water. Some salamanders that live on land and climb trees can grasp the bark with their tail. Still other salamanders use their tails when attracting a mate or for storage of food.

Fireflies, also called lightening bugs, do not have a real tail. What they do have is a special tip at the end of their abdomen that they can light up. When we want to say "hello" to someone who is not right next to us, we wave to them. When a firefly wants to say "hello" to another firefly, it flashes the tail-like tip of its body. There are many kinds (species) of fireflies, and most are active at night when they cannot see each other very well. A firefly can light up the tip of its body and turn it on and off like a flashlight to signal to another firefly. Each species of firefly has a certain pattern of flashes that it uses, so even in the dark fireflies can tell if they have found another firefly like themselves. Males and females of the same species flash back and forth to each other if they want to get to know each other better.

Some bats don't have tails. But most do. In some species, the tail extends beyond the skin (membrane) that connects its thighs. This looks something like a mouse's tail. Sometimes these bats use their tails to feel their way as they back into a crack. In other species, the tail runs just to the edge of the membrane. Whether a bat's tail is short or long, the bat uses it to take off into the air, to fly, to change direction while flying, and to sweep prey up into its mouth.

A North American river otter's tail is about one-third the length of its body. It is very long, very wide and very muscular. An otter uses its tail to help it swim fast through the water. It also uses its tail to steer when swimming slowly and to help prop itself up when it is standing on its hind legs.

These are all physical adaptations.

To Holly, my lifelong friend.—MH

Thanks to Education Staff at Walking Mountains Science Center (Avon, CO) for verifying the accuracy of the information in this book.

Translated into Spanish: *Las colas de los animales*

Lexile® Level: AD770L

key phrases: physical adaptations, tails

Animals in this book include (in order of appearance): red squirrel (cover), snapping turtle (title page), common garter snake, green frog tadpole, white-tailed deer, beaver, striped skunk, Virginia opossum, red fox, bald eagle, muskrat, downy woodpecker, porcupine, honey bee, and tortoise beetle.

Bibliography:
Holland, Mary, and Chiho Kaneko. Naturally curious: a photographic field guide and month-by-month journey through the fields, woods, and marshes of New England. North Pomfret, VT: Trafalgar Square , 2010. Print.

Cataloging Information is available through the Library of Congress.

Library of Congress Cataloging in Publication Control Number: 2017018954

978-1-628559767	English hardcover
978-1-628559774	English paperback
978-1-628559781	Spanish paperback
978-1-628559798	English ebook downloadable
978-1-628559804	Spanish ebook downloadable

Interactive, read-aloud ebook featuring selectable English (9781628559811) and Spanish (9781628559828) text and audio (web and iPad/tablet based)

Manufactured in China, June 2017
This product conforms to CPSIA 2008
First Printing

Arbordale Publishing
Mt. Pleasant, SC 29464
www.ArbordalePublishing.com